The Fire Thief

A Life in Poems

JUDITH KOLL HEALEY

Minneapolis, Minnesota

CALUMET EDITIONS

Minneapolis, Minnesota

Second Edition December 2022

The Fire Thief. Copyright © 2021 by Judith Koll Healey
All rights reserved.

No part of this book may be used or reproduced by any means, graphic, electronic or mechanical, including photocopying, recording, taping or by any information storage retrieval system, without the written permission of the publisher except in the case of brief quotations embodied in critical articles and reviews.

10 9 8 7 6 5 4 3 2
ISBN: 978-1-959770-74-9

Cover design by Gary Lindberg
Book design by Christopher Chambers

The Fire Thief

For Cole, Finnian, Sofia, Frank, Eva, Beatrice,
Harriet, Anna and Lucy

Donc le poète est vraiment voleur de feu…si ce qu'il rapporte de là-bas a forme, il donne forme; si c'est informe, il donne de l'informe.

The Poet is really a stealer of fire…If what he brings back from over there has form, he gives it form; if it is unformed, he gives it unformedness.

—Arthur Rimbaud, (letter to Paul Demeny, May 15, 1871)

Also by Judith Koll Healey

The Canterbury Papers
The Rebel Princess
Frederick Weyerhaeuser and the American West

Contents

Part One: Girl

Secrets   2
The Picture Window   4
Falling Through Time   6
On Tuesday I Noticed the Ghosts   7
There is Nothing Like a Dame   8

Part Two: Young Wife

Night-Song   10
Room Service   12
Wife   13

Part Three: Young Mother

Family Summer Circus   16
Foreigners   18
Nine Years Old   20
Summer Again   22

Part Four: Working Mother

Forgotten Bread   24

Part Five: Traveler

Airport Farrago 28
Losing It (or Paul Travels With His Aging Parents) 30
The Oracle on Delfi 32
The Korae at the Acropolis Museum 33
Leaving Villefranche sur Mer 34

Part Six: Daughter

Mother at Seventy-three 36

Part Seven: Sister

Ode to My Brother at Seventy-five 38

Part Eight: Friend

Her Friend Lay Dying in a Distant City 42
In Memoriam 43
Fourth of July 44
Moving On 46
After the Wedding Party 48

Part Nine: Older Wife

A Love Poem from an Older Wife 50

Part Ten: Poet

The Fire Thief 52

PART ONE: GIRL

Secrets

There are secrets   in childhood
which are now hidden   from us all
under the front porch swims
the dank smell of earth, bones   secrets
have simmered.

In the corner of her mind
lurk ribbons of color
she could once seize   Only
those bright bones and bee-jars
feckless birds with swathed wings
who could not be saved
heaped high

And other bits   Oh, yes
air gusts   even in secret places
earth spoke quietly but the sun rang out!
every toe mattered   when it touched
warm cement   Fingers danced

In the Spring the water   (oh, yes)
ran through the melting snow   and no other
sound mattered.   Late in the summer
leaves whispered love to the dark   and
in the Fall they crackled in protest underfoot
The advent chant of white death to come.

Secrets

Reach back with swollen fingers of memory
toward the brightness
grasp the green dreams and cool dirt
and wind melodies of childhood   and feel
that dear once-you
with secrets

The Picture Window

In the fashionable 'fifties
when Youngstown kitchens gleamed
from magazine pages everywhere

And Beaver Cleaver's mother
wore high heels in the kitchen
my mother fell in love with

Picture windows   those angles
that broad rectangular sweep
of glass that had never been

Or at least not in Minnesota
available to the common folk
was now her personal obsession

And so my patient father
ordered one for our dining room
so that we could all look out

My brother and I watched a whole wall
break apart   only to be sealed again
with the frame that held the magic glass.

Look   a miracle of the open
now we could sit at Sunday dinner
mid-day, with mashed potatoes always

And observe the lawn, the sidewalk,
the quiet elm shaded street outside
punctuated by an occasional Chevy

The Picture Window

But as I watched out one day   it
occurred to me that passersby
my playmates or our neighbors

Could look in on us as well
at the four of us strung like beads
around our square, linen covered table

And the puzzle that arose
in my child's mind was this:

Was the picture framed
the outside world?
Or was it us?

Falling Through Time

She fell through time
Already at eight years.
Round child face shone
With the light of the sky

Each cheek held the sun
And the gold of earth's flowers
Lined her swinging hair

Lying on her back, warm
Ground beneath her   she saw
The clouds smile back

At twelve years things changed
Blood ran as her new self
Unwound   Her mother said
'You are a woman now'

Then she cried out   No! Not yet…
And she threw herself on
The warm grass and watched
The clouds while time paused
And passed.

On Tuesday I Noticed the Ghosts

...they were waiting for me at the supermarket   peering at me quietly at first   then some began to murmur and the sound swelled behind me up and down the aisles   following me all the way to the produce counter—Oxydol, Swansdown, Ovaltine, Postum—all right, what do they want from me?   And I pack them carefully in a brown paper sack   a mountain of ghosts inside pay for them and carry them home to my own kitchen and I remember now my grandmother drank postum in another time when I was some other, smaller person   and she was large to me with a long braid of steel down her back which she unwound at night dropping a million hairpins like used stars on the dresser and my brother and I watching—oh—at her stocky back wondering how did our father ever?   and it was my aunt who used Oxydol and Swansdown and—oh—with an ache I am again in her kitchen as she appears with a wicker basket of wet clothes arising from the basement which hums with a life of its own   when the laundry is finally on the line, starched petticoats hanging in a choir practicing stiffness for church   and we girls have all washed our hair with Halo shampoo, we sit again at night in the kitchen   she bending over a needle instructing me or my cousins on the tasks women perform like birds in a quiet forest   and crickets playing on the edge of town two blocks away   and red ore dust from my uncle's work clothes settling in the back hall   and I clutch at the very ordinariness of the ticking kitchen clock still grateful for that peace which is now a ghost to me.

There is Nothing Like a Dame

    She is almost alone in the house
        Baby Jane asleep in the back bedroom
          South Pacific LP on the phonograph
            Chorus of sailors singing "There is nothing
              Like a Dame!" and she wants to move with
                  The rise and fall of the melody and the rousing
                    Chant of men wanting women and she can
                    Whirl and dance to all the rhythms and sounds
                    And feel free so she flings herself about
                      All the time watching   her reflection
                      In the mirror over the mantel
                    While surfing on the wave of
                        Sound and feeling and knowing
Nothing
                      Of what it all means.

Part Two: Young Wife

Night-Song

The scarred   double-hung windows
are open to the sultry summer air
and the sound of crickets rising

In the bedroom she waits for the car
a distant sound at first   then closer
the motor finally grunting to a halt

Her heart hurts from something
she can't quite name it
that has flown from her marriage

Outside lurks the heavy night
coiled around closed flowers
an August fist around her mind

Even in bed she feels the still heat
beating on her with dark blows
the sky seen through the window

Pock-marked with grinning stars
So many nights she waits
just like this night

His missing face floating
behind her closed eyelids
the image pulled long by creeping

Fingers of sleep   drawing all down
as she battles to stay awake

Night-Song

Finally　she breathes out
buckles her bones about her
and slips into her dreams
still seeking that absent face

Room Service

1.
Though stretched out full length
covering the bed with her body
her memory is that she is curled
huddled in the dark room's corner
shadows playing on the wall
traffic wah-wahing outside.
cornered, knowing he is coming
knowing the dream just interrupted
will never return.

2.
You have it wrong, the hotel
is first cabin and the woman
never was taken or pressed
into service   and the wait
is for the breakfast ordered
the night before and how

could she know   except that
she does and the waiting
frightens her all the same.

Wife

a slap
no more than
to kill a mosquito
between hand
and cheek

particles of life
fall from the skies
rearrange themselves
over me like
a new quilt

everything
changed
in a minute.

Part Three: Young Mother

Family Summer Circus

Boys smile   eyes apple-bright,
a hustle and a fast two step through the kitchen
out the back door two-three-four
whirling off into the sky in imaginary chariots

To be deposited by The Force
hot and sweaty as interplanetary interlopers
promptly at six o'clock

The moral mother shovels them away from the television
'Aw mom, not a family dinner again.'
     'Shut up, two-three-four' said
the mother, doing her own fast two step
around the smiling sink

'Tickets to the circus free   sold
     right here' said the Ringmaster father
martialing the loud dusty bodies
around the innocent table.
We drop into a collective space with a sigh
and a prayer to the day

Summer chatter falls on heat   and
wild words rise good-naturedly
A show in every ring and some on the side
with monkeys and dwarfs applauding
Everyone talks   No one listens

Ah   some day   when I am old and alone at table
I will remember summers and boy-noise

Family Summer Circus

will call to mind the family two-step
and the circus where everyone starred...

—In homage to Ronsard
Quand vous serez bien vielle...Sonnets for Helen, 1587

Foreigners

My son leans
forward on
the kitchen table

chin on sturdy arm
sun lighting down
wedging his lip

'I think I'll ask
dad to teach me
how to shave'

Hope lights his
tan face familiar
territory a mirror

Of my own   then
a flick of light
passes over him

Out of his body
grows another
an unfamiliar jaw

A body too large
heavy shoulders
a man emerges

Another flick
the shutter snaps
the man is gone.

Foreigners

We step out of
one another
the boy   from me

The man   from him
our boundaries
taking shape

I watch the sun
shift slowly across
his face and then

I know I am
another country
from him.

Nine Years Old

The starry gauze of my love
Surrounds you   a shroud of life.
You wake   sleep-breath sweetly
Mixing with murmurs of
Half-baked cakes of dreams.

Oh child   Trusting tell
Your recent night visions
And I will hold them carefully
In the vessel of my heart

What price would I pay
   Mother-rich as I am
To spin that gauze-shield perfectly

So no evil could spear through
No gun-sword-word could harm
That sweaty-sweet-breathed dreamer

No midnight jangle of the telephone
Car screeching or falling airplane
Or creeping quiet inner blackness
Would slice my shield
And it would never fade.

Yet even as the blossoms of my love
Color the air and warm the sun
Time rustles ominously between us
And   shadows lurk in the corner.

Nine Years Old

Oh, child! One day
My mother-curve of love
Over your sleeping body
Will melt with age
And you will lie alone

Summer Again

Summer again
Time passes over us
Bringing the violent rains
And summer again.

All the same   but different.
Rows of roses and yellow marigolds
Dot the window   and the boys
All the same   race past.

Larger than last summer
Sprouting hair like grass
Changed somehow over winter
 Still on the edge of childhood
Larger but all the same.

Blonde cubs whaling through the house
Strewing wanton energy and sun
Of their own   No longer children

Summer again
Green spreads over lawns
Tan colors the boys' faces
And it is all the same as last year
But different.

Part Four: Working Mother

Forgotten Bread

My public self
wears a business suit
sits at meeting
a solemn bird perched
on a pew at High Mass

It's tricky   this morning
my mind wandering   slipped
down the page   pulling the numbers
into a blur   pulling them
off the page   slipping
into my other self

Where have I left
the children? Are they
lost   misplaced in the maze
the funhouse of memory

Like a good wife
I furiously sweep the floor
the closet...searching for
the children
Out tumble braids, scarred knees   caps
band-aids, model cars   dead tennis shoes
alphabet books with covers
of green, silent crocodiles
teeth glinting ominously
but no children.

Did I forget the carpool
leave them standing alone
with rain streaming over them
in sad, grey ribbons   other mothers
already come and gone
in station wagons   packed
with luckier found children?

Did I knead the bread?
or is it, too   forgotten
on the kitchen counter

Soft and white   growing
rising recklessly in the sun
billowing over the rim of
the pan like a mad sail
conquering its boat
Growing over the edges
of the counter   covering cupboards
refrigerator   range   floor
taking over

Will the children
running in from school
finally carried home by some other
child's kind and generous mother
run into the soft, white death
of the bread
I forgot to knead?

Part Five: Traveler

Airport Farrago

faces
swept together
autumn leaves

blowing past
as i sit
in the airport

one face
a friend
i knew her once

i lean forward
to speak   and see
it is not her

and i know
suddenly
i am not

the face
she would have
known

the face
returns
fragments

in a dream
puzzle pieces
raining over me

Airport Farrago

they fall into
place   a crazy-
quilt

a pattern of mistakes
only the chin
and the right cheek

the nose and
half an eye
are young

the red hair
autumn leaves
only partly living

half green half dead
a blizzard of pieces
now come together

but the picture
the face
a confusion

i hold
the looking glass
upside down

now i see
it is myself

Losing It
(or Paul Travels with His Aging Parents)

I left the toothpaste in Paris
but it was almost finished   the
shampoo in the Bordeaux hotel.

I left my sunglasses on a table
in Volos   but found them on return.
Socks in Aegina   a shirt in Athens

My belongings strewn on a trail
across Europe. And finally
on Delfi where mystery swirls

I lost the sweater I loved.
It was new from France and
never worn—it simply disappeared

Was not there at some point
my son Paul said it was hard
for him to see his parents losing

it   I've lost my heart to
France   lost memories of sunsets
to Greece, lost visions of

Sun waltzing with water   paths
of sunlight and ink blue   lost these
to the islands   ferried away by time

Losing It (or Paul Travels with His Aging Parents)

Fragments of memory   of mind
of poems come and gone   of
half-hearted attempts to hold on

Scatter in the winds of my wake
Paul is right indeed   Every
day is a process of losing it.

The Oracle on Delfi

I saw a man die on Delfi   struck
by the gods for his impiety, but
I may be crazed or mistaken.

The signs warn in five languages
watch your cigarettes — Danger
of fire.   But this man carelessly

tosses his cigarette   then he seems to
slip on the stones and fall
bringing down the mountain as he dies

A shadow descends like a shroud
but when the sun splits it
I see the man again   climbing above

Later a thousand bees buzz near
the stadium   but none are ever seen.
running water rushes above the theatre

But no mountain brook appears
Man carries his own sacred deep
within himself   senses and memories

that wrap the heart   if he does
not nurture these murmuring shadows
to life   neither will Apollo

The Korae at the Acropolis Museum

Those old Greeks got some things right
choosing the persistence of marble
to send their message ahead

See the Korae standing still
white votives washed in time
forming a bracelet around Athena

Each silent witness strains for voice
staring out over coiling braids
left leg slightly forward

as if stepping into the future
Each wears the same unearthly smile
of a most amusing private thought

I wait for a signal from those blind eyes
to my own   wait for the mystery-driven
smiles to flicker   wait for any sign at all

That they recognize a sister

Leaving Villefranche sur Mer

Take the bright red buttons of geraniums
waving in the wind on the balcony
welcoming any viewer to full life

Take also the blue bay beyond
where tiny white sails dot the water
like the dotted swiss of my childhood dresses

And the hills   mounting over the bay
offering up miraculous cypress and other
green trees straight out of Corniche rock

Interspersed with creamy villas and hosting
roads running like happy ribbons over arches
inspired by Caesar's engineers

Every vista calls the soul to its own
memory of life's beauty, even
those from long ago   like a window

Opening onto innocence   where the viewer
who sees the golden sun setting on waves
captures the vision forever in her heart.

Part Six: Daughter

Mother at Seventy-three

A slim bone under sterile sheets
You   lie on the hospital bed
your body curved sideways   as if
to make a statement about your life

Years of angry words float between us
pushing us apart   extending the
boundaries of our universe

Curds and whey of early nursery rhymes
read in the safety of a child's bed
have soured in the shared tick of the clock

Particles of the past gather and sting
tears begin a journey somewhere
inside me   like a river they rise

Flowing through a forest thick with
arguments   broken trust   hurt
feelings scattered like autumn leaves

We were a cosmic mis-match
you did not see me   nor the paths
I must choose leading away from you

If the clock turned its face to the east
and our travels together began anew
it would be   the same

it would be
the same

Part Seven: Sister

Ode to My Brother at Seventy-five
(with apologies for scanning and corny rhymes)

Larry's always been my brother
He was born first
but coming second in the family
gave me quite a thirst.

I tried to copy all the things
that Larry did so well
but I was never quite as good
and playing football was hell!

At Regis, Cretin and Cotter too
in high school Larry was best
and he earned an award at St. John's U
Student of the Year, ahead of the rest.

He practiced law for many years
and in politics he proved 'yes-he-can'
I had to work to forgive him that
because he had turned out Republican!

Like many of us he sowed some wild oats
long ago in his turbulent youth
but now he's been sober for 31 years
and you can see he's no longer uncouth.

Ode to My Brother at Seventy-five

Despite his success in his worldly endeavors
his family always came out on top
Kirkie, Dani and Matt are stars
and his love for Susan will never stop.

So here's cheer to Larry, his children and wife
I've been lucky to have him as brother.
He's been good and kind to me all of my life
I would never want any other!

Part Eight: Friend

Her Friend Lay Dying in a Distant City

When she heard the news she thought
I will rise up and go to him.
I am a princess of his past

In the distant city concrete canyons
Surround the sterile box where, it is said,
He still   even now   lies breathing

She would rise up and go to him
Riding through the canyons in
A rented pumpkin   she was once his princess

At the ancient hotel she hears
Unmistakably the brilliant sound of
A Rachmaninoff   piano crescendo.

The music enters into her with power
And bitterness for all the joys of life
That he would no longer share.

Cascading notes fire through her
Where all past pleasures filtered now by
Sheets of grief   would forever burn

One day the Swan will also call
Her name in a high clear voice
Then she will move forward in line

And pass through the door
As the steam of death
Melts all memories

In Memoriam

She was a friend.
By her nature
Like a highly strung
Animal   a fox or
A young colt   She
Said once her heart's
Desire was to
Sing like a bird
And fly like Peter Pan

When the airplane broke
Apart and her keen
And beautiful spirit
Was released   surely
A white, subtle body
Formless but luminous
Against the night sky
Sang as it flew
Into our common memory.

—for Judith Delouvrier

Fourth of July

bad news
static
like firecrackers
rolls over
telephone wires
bad static
it is

bad news
you dying
it is
old friend
you were

once a child
sitting in a field
hooded by night
I was

I heard
static crackling
I saw
umbrellas of light

blues, yellows,
greens sprinkling
colored parachutes
on the sky
they were

Fourth of July

I drew
my breath
to see
the lights
erase
the noise

and I wish
I were
that child
again

and that
those lights
would follow
this   noise
I do.

Moving On

We watch the house fold itself
into boxes   twenty-six years
it takes a heap of living to make
a house a home and all folding

into boxes   my father is dying
is anxious he whispers when
I bend my ear down to his mouth
that has proclaimed poems for
ninety-six years   is anxious

about the move, the house, the
home   not about dying but
about our move   our house
our home

Gone with the Wind   he whispers
about himself   the fire in
our new house erupts   alarms
ringing   our not-yet-home
delayed   we hover overland

bunking with friends   uprooted
feeling like the garbage ship
roaming the world looking for
a home   surely children of
this twentieth century

Hildegarde says all will be well.
bells will ring   all will be well.
all things pass   moving   dying,
and always new life.

—for Doc Meany

After the Wedding Party

The sun has died   the music has faded
and the stars salt all the dark sky.

We straggle up the path to the carpark
the river murmuring at our heels

As if to say…don't go yet, don't go yet.
but we push on, away from the song

Our own children lead   grown now   smoking
cigars   drinking champagne and parenting us

Mellowed by wine   having feasted and danced
off guard one might say in our cheer

I almost fail to notice how bound we are
encircled by a long chain of common memories

Failed marriages   alcohol- soaked lives   children cut
dead in the encroaching violence of our time

Shared shadows dance on the fringe of our little party
like the evening fog that rises where we step

So moved am I by these ghosts that
minutes later when we part   I cannot say

If it is the pain of being together
 or the pain of separating

That over-takes me

Part Nine: Older Wife

A Love Poem from an Older Wife

If there were many more worlds
        known to us
Each with its own moon
        owning millions of stars
Each with its own seas
        fully dotted with mountains
And every one of these worlds
        held countless people
People just like us
        men and women
And they crowded the galaxies
        whizzing on spaceships
Each world connected to the others
        and all of the faces
Known to many others
        the busyness of trillions
Even so, in that mad universe
        we would have found each other.

Part Ten: Poet

The Fire-Thief

When Prometheus stole the fire
    from the gods
He wasn't kidding around

  Tired of men who were beetles
    snuffling and shuffling
  Noses to the ground for crumbs

  When he brought the fire back
    they gathered 'round
  Heads lifting for the first time

  In wonder they stretched
    out their hands for a share
  Swallowing the fire whole

  They embraced the warm
    shedding their shells
  And stood upright with life

  Now they saw color and
    words and music and love
  Swept over them like new winds

  The first song was born   the first
    poem was written
  No woman would never be the same again

And the gods looked down on
    the laughter and love
And muttered among themselves.

Acknowledgements

Several of these poems were previously published in *Studio One*, *Milkweed Chronicle* and *Groundwater*.

Thanks to Helene deJong Taylor in Paris for her assistance on the accurate quotation from Arthur Rimbaud.

Thanks to my family and close friends for providing so many years of these events, happy and sad, and so many years of affection, which is what makes life worthwhile.

—Judith Koll Healey

About the Author

Judith Koll Healey writes and lives in Minneapolis, Minnesota. She has published several novels set in medieval France and a biography of a notable founder of Minnesota's lumber industry. Healey is also an occasional contributor to the Op Ed pages of the *Minneapolis StarTribune*, where she writes on politics and culture.

www.ingramcontent.com/pod-product-compliance
Lightning Source LLC
Chambersburg PA
CBHW020254090426
42735CB00010B/1926